# TV TIME '79

### by PEGGY HERZ

## SCHOLASTIC BOOK SERVICES
NEW YORK • TORONTO • LONDON • AUCKLAND • SYDNEY • TOKYO

Copyright © 1979 by Scholastic Magazines, Inc. All rights reserved. Published by Scholastic Book Services, a division of Scholastic Magazines, Inc.

12 11 10 9 8 7 6 5 4 3 2 1          1          9/7 0 1 2 3 4/8

Printed in the U.S.A.                                      11

# Contents

# ☆ Lou Ferrigno: ☆
# From 148-lb. Weakling to
# *The Incredible Hulk*

Watch out for David Banner when he gets angry. He turns into The Incredible Hulk! The Hulk is a huge, green monster who howls in rage. *Nothing* stands in his way!

I went to see the Hulk not long ago. *The Incredible Hulk* was in production at Universal Studios in California. It wasn't hard to find him. He was the only green monster around! "Hello," he said, holding out his big green hand. I took his hand and shook it carefully. The green didn't rub off and my hand didn't break. The Hulk was being gentle. Then I looked up — and up! — at the Hulk's green face. That face isn't the prettiest one you'll see on TV this season. But it's a face that stands out in any season! I gulped and smiled bravely.

1

On TV, the Hulk flies into towering fits of rage. But now, between scenes, he was smiling and relaxed. The Hulk is played by Lou Ferrigno. Lou had been at work since 6 A.M. During a break in the filming, he took time out to talk about himself — and about the seven-foot monster he plays in the CBS series.

Lou's own story is almost as incredible as the make-believe stories about *The Incredible Hulk*.

Life was never easy for Lou. When he was a child, he was very small and shy. "I grew up in Brooklyn, New York, where my father was a policeman," Lou told me. "When I was three years old, I had a bad ear infection. I lost part of my hearing because of that." The kids he knew in Brooklyn either teased him — or they ignored him. As he got older, he spent more and more time alone.

"My father wasn't too poor, but we were just getting by," he said of his early years. "Everything was a struggle. I went to Brooklyn Technical School. I liked gym, but I wasn't crazy about school. It was hard for me. I didn't talk much. I wanted to be a baseball player, but playing a major sport like that required hearing. I couldn't hear the crack of the bat. I was also very thin and I couldn't gain weight. I had some friends," he added, "but mostly I did everything on my own."

Lou's childhood was not very happy, but he isn't one to complain. "Nobody gave me anything," he said. "My parents had their own problems. I was on my own. That's why I tell kids that it's up to them to make something of themselves. There were many times when I felt discouraged. But I knew that if I stopped trying, that would be it. I couldn't hear well, but I could see and I could walk, so I figured I could be a lot worse off than I was."

One day when he was 15 years old, Lou was looking through magazines at a newsstand near his home. Suddenly he came across a magazine about body building and physical fitness. It pictured men with tremendous muscles and strength. Young Lou — all 5'8" and 148 pounds of him — read the magazine with interest. Then he went home and announced that he was going to start lifting weights in the basement. His family thought he was crazy.

"Everybody laughed and tried to discourage me," Lou said, "but I kept at it. I wanted to build up my strength and my health. But more important, I wanted to build *confidence* in myself. I wanted to give myself a sense of well-being. I read more and more magazines about how other people trained, and I changed my eating habits. Instead of eating ice cream and cake, I began to eat meat, fish, and eggs. I never imagined, though, that I would ever end up looking like those guys in the magazines!"

Gradually, he began to see results. "Now I'm 6'5" and weigh 275," he said with a smile. "I came to California to endorse body building products and do exhibitions. I didn't really think of being an actor. I thought I was too big!"

By that time, he had won all the major body building contests, including Mr. America, Mr. Universe, and Mr. World. Lou also appeared in a documentary film about body building called *Pumping Iron*.

"I'll always stay active in body building," he added. "When I was in school, people thought body building was for uncoordinated freaks. I think I've helped explode that myth. Kids today are more aware of the importance of eating properly than they used to be. I often talk to groups of young people. I tell them how important it is to keep their bodies in shape and to follow a good diet."

Lou also played professional football for a short time. "I played tackle for a team in Canada," he said. "I've always liked football and thought I wanted to play. But I didn't like the punishment your body takes during each game. I quit after three months."

But nothing he had done quite prepared him for the role of the Hulk. "It takes about two and a half

The Incredible Hulk being chased through a muddy swamp — which doesn't exactly soothe his violent temper!

hours for my make-up to be put on," he said. The make-up includes green skin ("One coat of make-up on my face, four coats on my body," Lou noted), special contact lenses for his eyes, false teeth clipped into his mouth, and a little putty on his nose.

"Wearing all that make-up isn't really much fun," Lou admitted. "But I enjoy playing the role — even though we work long, hard hours. I hope to go on in acting and play other roles."

At first, the producers of *The Incredible Hulk* hadn't planned on using two people in the starring role. They hired Bill Bixby, who played the role of mild-mannered David Bruce Banner very well. But Bill is not very tall. How were they going to turn him into a huge, raging, green monster? It took some thought before they came up with their solution. The starring role, they decided, would be shared by *two* actors: Bill Bixby as Banner and the towering Lou Ferrigno as the Hulk.

The solution turned out to be a good one. Bill is a very scholarly-looking David Banner. And he is very involved with the people around him. Usually he gets *too* involved, in fact, and finds himself in the middle of all kinds of situations and adventures which trigger his anger. Bill's calm and quiet appearance makes his change into the uncontrollable Hulk even more startling.

All of it is meant to be fun, and it is. The idea of

Before and After: Bill Bixby as the scholarly David Banner, and Lou Ferrigno as the steel-muscled Hulk.

being able to change ourselves into something we're not is an appealing idea. When David Banner gets angry, he turns into the Hulk. It's fantasy, and it's fun to watch.

Lou Ferrigno's *own* story isn't fantasy, however. He changed himself, and he did it in spite of the discouragement, even ridicule, of people.

Our interview came to an end. Lou's green face broke into a smile as he headed into the studio. It was time to turn into the incredible Hulk, the newest superman on TV.

## ☆ Quinn Cummings: ☆
## A New Kid Sister for Kristy McNichol in *Family*

This year *Family* added a new member. Eleven-year-old Quinn Cummings says about joining the cast of the popular ABC series: "The family has adopted me."

Quinn may be new to *Family*, but she's not new to acting. She's been working since she was eight. And last year she became one of the youngest people ever nominated for an Academy Award for her supporting role in *The Goodbye Girl*. She didn't win the award, but just being nominated was a big thrill. It's an honor bestowed on very few performers of *any* age.

I went to see Quinn one day at her home in the Hollywood Hills. She lives there with her mother, a dog, which is half coyote and half German shepherd, a cat named Pooh, and two hamsters in a fancy cage. Quinn had just gotten home from school when I arrived. She changed into faded shorts and a shirt and we settled down on the porch. From there, we could look down on all the houses nestled in the hills below. "I've lived in this house all my life," Quinn said. "We call it the blue blob because it's always been painted blue."

I asked Quinn how she got into acting.

"A neighbor of ours knew a children's agent," Quinn replied. "I went to see her and got a part in a TV commercial — for floor wax. My part was to scuff the floor!"

Quinn found that she liked working. "At one point, though, I didn't work for six months," she said. "Then I got a part in *The Six Million Dollar Man*. I was also in *Big Eddie* for 11 weeks and in *Baretta*, *Family*, and two movies-of-the-week. One of those movies was *Night Terror*," Quinn added with a shudder. "It gave me nightmares!"

Then Quinn paused and smiled. She was remembering one of the most exciting days of her life. "I was working on *Baretta* when the Oscar nominations were announced," she said. "My mother came to the set and told me that I had been nominated. I was really excited. I went to the award ceremonies. I wore a pink-and-white dress,

Quinn began her acting career in TV commercials. "I've done 15 commercials, and have tried out for many that I didn't get," she said. "It's hard when you don't get the job, but something else usually comes along."

pink ballet slippers, and pink socks. I was surprised that I was as calm and relaxed as I was."

Quinn loved being in *The Goodbye Girl*, she said. "Everybody in it helped me a lot," she added. "They were all very nice."

It's her mother, though, who has helped her the most over the years, Quinn said. "She takes me to interviews, gets my clothes back and forth, and does everything for me. You go on an interview and if you don't get the job, you have to lug all your stuff back home. If you *do* get the job, someone has to stay on the set with you—and there may not be any place for them to sit down. I've done 15 commercials," Quinn noted, "and have tried out for many that I didn't get. It's hard when you don't get the job, but something else usually comes along."

Quinn goes to regular school when she's not working. "I'm in the seventh grade," she told me. "My mother drives me down the hill and I take the bus from there. I like school. I take math, English, social studies — all the regular subjects. I especially like to read.

"None of the other kids in my school work. I regard my working as a hobby. It's something I enjoy doing. I'd quit if I didn't like it.

"My mother and I read a lot. I like to stay home. I'm a real homebody!" Quinn laughed. "When I do get together with my friends, we go shopping or we just talk. But none of them live nearby. Our mothers have to drive us to each other's houses. Here at home, I have things I have to do — like keep my room neat and keep the hamsters' cages clean.

"When I have time, I like to swim, roller skate, ice skate, and play any game involving running. I'm allowed to watch three hours of TV every day. I like *Barney Miller* and most of the top shows." Quinn paused for breath. It was very clear by now that she was a really busy person.

"I also love music," she added. "I play the piano and I take lessons in ballet, jazz, and disco dancing."

Annie and Buddy. When Annie was first adopted by the Lawrences, she irritated everyone — especially Buddy! Now Annie feels at home and Buddy is delighted with her new "sister."

Now she's working in a popular TV series that could mean a great deal to her career. Her older "sister" on the show is played by Kristy McNichol, one of Hollywood's most popular young actresses.

Kristy is 16 now and has really grown up on TV. I first met her when she was 14, and she was somewhat gangly. But only a year later, she had grown tall and stunning, and had won an Emmy for her role as Buddy Lawrence in *Family*. She had also signed contracts to do TV movies for CBS and a drama special for NBC.

Kristy comes from a show business family. Her mother Carollyne was once an actress; her 17-year-old brother Jimmy is an actor. It all began because Carollyne often took her kids to the set with her when she was working. Kristy and Jimmy were five and six then, and they learned early to be quiet or they'd get thrown off the set. They also learned something else. Acting looked like fun! They wanted to try it too. Their mother helped them get jobs doing commercials, and they were off to a good start. Commercials led to small parts in several TV shows — and the parts kept getting bigger and bigger.

Kristy starred in several "ABC Afterschool Specials," including *Me and Dad's New Wife* and *The Pinballs*. The books from which these specials were made are offered by Arrow Book Club. *Me*

Doug Lawrence has a heart-to-heart talk with Buddy.

*and Dad's New Wife* is called *A Smart Kid Like You*. *The Pinballs* is being offered by the club this year for the first time.

Kristy was a guest on *Starsky and Hutch* and *The Bionic Woman* and other TV shows. People began to notice her. She was still a "kid," but she was also an *actress* with a genuine, natural talent. Kristy never took acting lessons. She just seemed to know how to show feelings and emotions.

No one could be sure when she started how long her success would last, though. Her mother had once pointed out to me that Hollywood is filled with children who get acting jobs for a few years. Then they reach 15 or 16 and there aren't many jobs for them. They are at an awkward age — too old to play children's roles, too young to play adults. Kristy has made it over the hurdle. She has turned 16 and her career is going stronger than ever.

Much of the money Kristy earns is being invested in real estate. Carollyne McNichol handles her children's investments. "The way I've invested their money," she said, "they'd never have to work again. We know that in this business you can be up one minute and down the next."

Kristy and Jimmy are trying to make sure that doesn't happen to them. They released their first record last spring — and that could open up a whole new career for them. Kristy wishes she had

The latest Lawrence family portrait: (left to right) Nancy (Meredith Baxter-Birney), Kate (Sada Thompson), Willie (Gary Frank), Buddy (Kristy McNichol), Annie (Quinn Cummings), and Doug (James Broderick).

more free time, but her chances of getting it are slim.

Both Kristy and Quinn are hard at work on *Family* now. Both of them hope their acting careers will be zipping along for many years to come. There is little doubt that they are a talented twosome, and are important to the success of *Family*.

## ☆ Nicholas Hammond ☆
## Spins a Magic Web in
## *The Amazing Spider-Man*

TV's newest fantasy hero leaps through the air on a magic web hidden in his wrist band. He crawls up and down buildings like an insect. He fights crime and protects the innocent. Who is he? The Amazing Spider-Man, of course!

He is played on TV by Nicholas Hammond, who has two roles in CBS's *The Amazing Spider-Man*. Nicholas plays Spider-Man and he plays Peter Parker. They are the same person — but not really the same. Here's how it happened:

Peter is a young science student and part-time news photographer. One day, he is bitten by a radioactive spider in a college laboratory. Suddenly, he has superhuman powers. He has become Spider-Man.

Nicholas Hammond as Peter Parker — a quiet, studious young man, until danger threatens. Then he becomes the Amazing Spider-Man!

No one is more puzzled by the sudden powers than Peter himself. Peter was always a shy, studious, non-violent young man. Now he is forced to lead a double life and he can share his secret with no one.

*Spider-Man* didn't start the season as a weekly series. But Spider-Man is scheduled to spin his web periodically throughout the year, luring TV viewers into his world of fantasy.

"I think people like the show," Nicholas said, "because they know the good guy will win in the end. They know they will see an exciting story filled with a lot of action, and they'll get involved with Peter... and with the super powers of Spider-Man."

Nicholas didn't read *Spider-Man* comics as a kid, but he's gotten to know the character well — both characters, in fact. "I can relate to many things about Peter Parker," he said. "Peter is shy and so was I. I think that's why I liked being on stage as a kid. Peter is a nice guy. If he hadn't been bitten by a spider, nobody would ever had heard of him. He is a very unremarkable guy — except that he is genuinely nice. He's the kind of guy who would join the Peace Corps to help other people."

For Nicholas, playing the two roles has been an exciting challenge — one he has been preparing for since his first role, when he was 10½ years old.

Nicholas' mother is also an actress. She was appearing on the London stage during World War II when Nicholas' father, then an aide to General Eisenhower, saw her performance and started courting her. They were married when the war ended. Nicholas was born in Washington, D.C. and lived there for six years. Then the family moved to Europe.

Nicholas saw his first stage play when he was eight. "It was in London and I'd never seen anything like it," he exclaimed. "I decided right then that I wanted to be an actor. It seemed so magical to me. I couldn't believe my eyes!"

The family returned to Washington two years after that, and six months later, Nicholas got his first acting job.

"Getting the job was a stroke of luck," Nicholas remembered. A movie called *Lord of the Flies* was being cast, and they needed 30 boys for it. The producer of the film lived in Washington, so they ran an ad in the newspaper, asking for boys, ages 10-13, who could speak with an English accent and would like to spend the summer filming a movie in Puerto Rico. It took me about 14 minutes to answer that ad! Being in that movie was a wonderful experience. We weren't paid very much, but I loved every minute of it."

The following year, when he was 11, Nicholas

first appeared in a play on Broadway in New York. His mother stayed in New York with him while he was working. "And my father and brother came up from Washington on weekends," he said, "My mother had mixed feelings about my acting. She was always supportive, but she never pushed me or made me feel it was something I should do. Her attitude was: If you enjoy acting, fine."

Nicholas traveled a great deal with road show companies of plays. Since he was too young to travel alone, his mother traveled with him. "Once when I was 14," he recalled with a laugh, "I felt I was too old to have my mother around. I was doing *The Happiest Millionaire* on Broadway with Walter Pidgeon. Then, when it came time to take it on the road, I just didn't want my mother along. But there was a little part in the play of a maid, so my mother took that part. Most people didn't know she was my mother."

Nicholas admitted that his childhood was anything but normal. While other kids were out playing, he was working. "Acting really took most of my time," he said. "But I loved it! It was the most wonderful childhood I could ever imagine. It gave me a chance to be around the most creative people in Hollywood and New York. I was living the life I wanted — and I was making money. But I saw other child performers who hated their lives. They

Spider-Man crawls up the side of a building — looking more like a spider than a man! Spider-Man's wall-climbing talents and magic webs help him capture dangerous criminals.

probably hadn't wanted to act in the first place. Some of them ended up being in the movies when they would rather have been outside playing with their friends.

"When I wasn't working, our life at home was totally normal. We used to travel as a family and go on picnics and do all those kinds of things. That changed a little after I was in the movie, *The Sound of Music*. That movie was such a huge hit that I became a mini-celebrity in my neighborhood. And when you're 14, you're not sure you want everybody staring at you!"

"Do you have any advice for other young people who would like to become actors?" I asked Nicholas. He smiled and thought about the question for a moment.

"For me, the business was wonderful," he answered. "But it's not something I would recommend for everyone — unless you feel it is the *only* thing you want to do. I would say to kids: If you want to act, do it on the local level — in your junior high drama department or in a community theater. Just bury yourself in acting and see if it's what you want. Many cities around the country have fabulous theater groups. Just make sure it's what you want to do. And let things happen naturally, one step at a time."

## ☆ Ron Glass: ☆
## The Cool Detective Harris in
## *Barney Miller*

For five seasons, Ron Glass has played Detective Harris in ABC's hit show, *Barney Miller*, one of the funniest shows on TV. All kinds of people wander into the station house of the 12th Precinct in New York. Many of them are as off beat as the stories they tell. Barney Miller and his detectives listen to them all. They listen with professional dedication — and with a sense of humor!

Detective Harris is the well-dressed, well-spoken member of Barney Miller's team. There may be craziness going on all around him, but he remains cool, calm, and unruffled, above it all — most of the time.

Playing Harris, said Ron, "is becoming more and more interesting. He has more 'flesh and blood' than he had when we started. He has developed as a character."

And as a person too, we might add. So have all the other members of TV's 12th Precinct: Barney himself (Hal Linden), Wojehowicz (Max Gail), Yemana (Jack Soo), and the rest. Their real human qualities are a big factor in the show's continued success.

Has success changed Ron Glass? He smiled at the question. "No," he answered, "success hasn't changed me very much, except that now I can afford things I couldn't afford before. But the more money you make, the more bills you have. Money doesn't really change the facts. You just have a more expensive car, a house instead of an apartment, a dog instead of a hamster." Ron laughed and added, "I have a dog named The Contessa. She thinks she's a queen! She's a little snooty and she makes no bones about it.

"I moved into a house in Hollywood Hills about a year ago," he said. "I bought some furniture for it, but not too much. I find myself staying home more now than I used to. I'm content to be alone."

Ron plays a New York City cop, but he is a midwesterner by birth. He was born in Evansville, Indiana, the youngest of five children of Crump and Lethia Glass. "There were four boys and one girl in my family," he told me. "I was on my own a

27

lot because I was so much younger than the others. My parents separated when I was one year old, so my mother raised us by herself. She was an important influence on all of us.

"We all worked," Ron explained. "I used to sell boxes of candy and I returned old bottles for the deposits. And I'll never forget collecting wagons full of newspapers to take to the paper-stock place to sell. I'd get three wagons filled and think I was really going to make some money — and I'd get two cents! Later, I worked at a plastics factory, and we all helped around the house. We all had chores to do. Since I was the youngest," Ron added with a smile, "I always had to clean the bathrooms.

"We were poor, but we had the essentials. I can't remember ever being hungry. We lived in housing projects in apartments made out of cardboard — or at least they seemed like they were!"

Ron had his dreams as a kid, but he didn't really know what he wanted to do with his life. "All I knew was that I didn't want to be like everybody else," he said. "I did well in school and I enjoyed sports. I was in one school play, but I didn't get involved in drama until college."

Ron won a scholarship to the university in his hometown. "In my freshman year, they were doing a play on campus, and they needed a black actor," he recalled. "There weren't many blacks in

Ron Glass plays the cool, always fashionable, detective Harris on *Barney Miller.*

the school. I was taking a speech course at the time, and the teacher asked me to read for the play. I did — and I won an award for that part!"

He gained more than that from being in the play, however. He gained a goal in life — to be an actor. After his college graduation, he headed for the Guthrie Theatre in Minneapolis. He spent four years there, learning his craft and performing in all kinds of plays. Finally, he decided it was time to move on. He went to Los Angeles.

"I arrived in Los Angeles on June 26, 1972," he recalled, smiling at the memory. "I moved into an $85 a month apartment that was next door to a beer company, across the street from a mortuary, and down the block from a cemetery. It was real cheery!" Ron grinned. "I worked for an answering service then, making $67.50 a week. I worked nights so I could go on interviews during the day. I got my first acting job at the end of that summer."

Producers Norman Lear and John Rich cast him in several of their hit shows, including *Sanford and Son*, *Maude*, and *Good Times*. Then he met Danny Arnold, who was casting an offbeat police show called *Barney Miller*.

It was offbeat because there was no violence. It was different — and its ratings were terrible. Ron and the others in the cast were starring in a big-time TV show, but nobody was watching them!

The detectives of New York City's 12th Precinct: (left to right) Harris (Ron Glass), Wojehowicz (Max Gail), Barney Miller (Hal Linden), Levitt (Ron Carey), Dietrich (Steve Landesburg), and Yemana (Jack Soo).

Nobody, that is, except for a few people who watched — and began to tell their friends about the show. Word-of-mouth reports began to spread. The show's ratings began to climb as more and more people tuned in. Now, it is one of the few long-running hits on TV. Many of the shoot-'em-up cop shows have disappeared while *Barney Miller* is still going strong.

Real-life policemen are among the show's biggest fans. One policeman wrote: "The working conditions and characters in your program are much like those in our office. We watch the show and laugh so much that it hurts!"

Ron himself wouldn't want to be a policeman in real life. "That kind of life would not appeal to me," he said. "Playing a detective on TV is enough for me!"

His role in *Barney Miller* has given Ron financial security. But that isn't his main reason for acting. "I need to know that I am doing my best," he said. "If I feel good about myself and my work from day to day, that's what's important. Someday, I would like to go back and work on the stage again. There are many roles I'd like to play."

Meanwhile, Ron Glass is happy being one of the stars of a hit TV show — one of the genuine, real-life shows that has lasted.

## ☆ Joyce DeWitt: ☆
# Childhood Dreams Come True with
# *Three's Company*

Joyce DeWitt was on crutches the day I met her. "I broke my toe," she explained with a smile. The crutches weren't slowing her down very much. She had just driven into Los Angeles from her apartment near the beach and she had a busy day planned.

Joyce is one of the stars of ABC's *Three's Company*. She plays the dark-haired Janet Wood in the show, which has become one of the biggest hits on TV.

"We get so much mail from kids," Joyce told me. "I think they like our show because of all the slapstick comedy we do. Somebody on the show is always getting slugged or falling down."

Joyce stars with John Ritter and Suzanne

Somers in the comedy hit. And she is still amazed by everything that has happened to her in the past year or so. "Working on the show makes sense to me," she admitted. "But then I go home and see the show on TV — and I feel like it's only being shown in my house! It's not like real TV to me!"

It is real TV, however, and its wacky humor has tickled the funny bones of TV viewers everywhere. For Joyce, it is a dream come true. She has wanted to be an actress since she was 13 years old and growing up in Speedway, Indiana, near Indianapolis.

"I was seven when we moved to Indiana from West Virginia, where I was born," Joyce recalled. "My dad found a job there working for a division of General Motors. He's a general foreman now." Joyce smiled, then added, "My dad is a real success story. He started life shoveling coal in a steel mill. Now he goes to work in a shirt and tie. He always had to work hard because he had a wife and four kids to feed!"

Joyce worked hard, too, especially in the speech and drama department of her high school. "Theater and music were my greatest loves," she said. "I was very lucky to have a teacher who was absolutely wonderful. His name was Donald Johnson; he was in charge of the speech and drama department at the school. I spent every free minute in

Starring in a hit show is a dream come true for Joyce DeWitt. "My dad always kidded himself that I would outgrow wanting to be an actress," she said, "but I never did."

workshops with him. I was in all the plays and in many speech contests around the area. He was angry when I became a cheerleader because it took time away from my work with him!"

Joyce loved everything about the stage — acting, singing, dancing, the works! "If you want to do something, you must do it," she believed then — and still does. "Classes are wonderful, but if you want to act, you must act — whether it's in school or in a community theater or wherever," she stressed.

Joyce's parents weren't so happy about their daughter's acting ambitions. Joyce can laugh about that now, but there were some touchy times when she was growing up. She remembers them well: "I was the only one in my family who was interested in show business and that really worried my father," she told me. "He wanted his two daughters to have security. By that, he meant getting an education, a teaching degree, and a husband with a good job. I got the teaching degree. I never planned to teach, but it gave him peace of mind."

After graduating from Ball State University in Muncie, Indiana, Joyce headed east to do summer stock. "I had planned all my life on going to New York and working on the stage," Joyce said. "I never even considered working in TV or movies. I thought you had to be beautiful to do them! I thought I would be creating a minor miracle if I worked on Broadway some day! But while I was doing summer stock, I met a guest director from UCLA in California. He talked me into going to UCLA to do graduate work in the theater. I arrived in California, took one look around, and decided to stay.

"I knew no one in California," Joyce admitted, "but that was a good time for me. It was a time of growth and new experiences and many changes. It was the first time I had really been on my own. I wasn't lonely. I made mistakes, but I learned. I studied with fine drama coaches while I was in graduate school. Gradually, people began to see me act, then they helped me meet other people. Things began to happen, though I spent two years getting absolutely NOWHERE. Only in the past two or three years did that begin to change."

She didn't see much of her family during those years, Joyce said. She was living in California; they were still back in Indiana. "I didn't have the plane fare home," she confided, "and I was too old for them to send me the fare! They would write and ask me, 'Did you get any work this week?' And my mother worried that I wasn't eating properly and so on." Joyce laughed sympathetically. It was clear that she felt very warm toward her concerned parents back home in Indiana.

Mrs. Roper offers a troubled trio comfort and sound advice.

"My dad always kidded himself that I would outgrow wanting to be an actress," she noted, "but I never did." Through the years, she worked as an actress and a director in summer stock and in small theaters. "I'd love to direct a film someday," she exclaimed. "I don't know enough to do that yet, but I'm going to learn!"

More then anything else, however, being in a hit TV show has changed her life. "I'm so thrilled by it all," she said with a big smile. "People watch our show and laugh. That's wonderful! The chances of a TV show getting and staying on the air are so slim — and having the show turn out to be a hit is just incredible! Two things have disappeared from my life because of the show's success," Joyce added. "I no longer have much free time — or privacy. When the show is in production, I spend several hours every night going over the script. It's not a matter of learning lines. It's a matter of creating a day in my character's life so that I understand what I'm doing and why I'm doing it. I work very hard at my craft."

Her efforts have paid off. The character of Janet Wood, the take-charge brunette member of *Three's Company*, is vital to the success of the show. "Janet is still growing up," Joyce said. "She has rough edges. She is still searching for her place in life. She doesn't have all the answers, but she

The cast of *Three's Company* celebrates a merry Christmas: (left to right) Mr. Roper (Norman Fell), Chrissy (Suzanne Somers), Mrs. Roper (Audra Lindley), Janet (Joyce DeWitt), and Jack (John Ritter).

sure is looking for them! I think of her as being independent, gutsy, and willing to try anything."

The same could be said of the actress who plays Janet Wood. Joyce DeWitt is filled with enthusiasm for the part, the show, and her life in general at the moment. "Fortunately, I broke my toe when the show was out of production," she said, "so I didn't miss any work."

Joyce has wanted to act since she was 13 years old. *Three's Company* has given her a chance to do that — and it may keep her busy for a long time.

## ☆ Haywood Nelson ☆
## Knows Exactly
## *What's Happening!!*

Haywood Nelson walked into the restaurant in Los Angeles with a big smile on his face. *What's Happening!!* was not in production at the time. Haywood had some free time, and he seemed to be enjoying himself. A young fan rushed up and asked him for his autograph. He gave it and then sat down at the table.

Haywood has become a big favorite of TV fans, especially young ones. Haywood plays the shy, innocent Dwayne in *What's Happening!!* Dwayne is the tag-along friend of Raj (Ernest Thomas) and Rerun (Fred Berry).

"I'm a *little* like Dwayne," Haywood said. "But I'd *never* do some of the things he does! Sometimes he is just *too* shy and *too* scared of the dark! I think he is changing, however. He is a little less shy than he used to be, and I like that. Being shy is okay, but he was ridiculous at first. The people doing the show also give me freedom to read the lines the way I want. And I can't do that without putting some of myself into the character."

Haywood is a veteran actor, even though he just turned 18 on March 25, 1978. He has been acting since he was five years old. Like so many performers, he got his show business start by doing TV commercials. "I did commercials from the time I was five until I was about 13," Haywood recalled. "During those years I also did some modeling for magazines."

Haywood grew up in New York City with his parents and his younger brother, Gary. "We were poor when I was growing up," Haywood told me. "My dad was working for an airline. We got along, but we lived in apartments in big housing projects and we wanted to live in a house. After I started doing commercials, my mother started working, too. She wanted to get us out of the city.

"I started school in P.S. 161 in New York," Haywood said. "Then, when I was in the fifth grade, we moved to Mineola, Long Island, which is just outside the city. I *loved* living out there. I could ride my bike, which I couldn't do in the city, and I could be outside all the time. Once we moved to Long Island, I was seldom home. I was always playing in the park."

Haywood loved playing with his friends. As he got older, however, he had little time for anything but work and school. By the time he was in junior high, he was a full-fledged actor, appearing in Mel Shavelson's play, *Mixed Company*, with Joe Bologna and Barbara Harris. Later, he spent a year on Broadway with Marlo Thomas in *Thieves*.

Every night when he was working on Broadway (and afternoons on matinee days), Haywood's father had to drive him into New York City and then come back later to pick him up. It wasn't an easy schedule for either one of them, Haywood admitted. "I'd get home about midnight and then have to get up and go to school the next day," he said. "I was always tired.

"I never took acting lessons," Haywood said. "I never thought about the future. I just did whatever came along. Everything happened so fast. I did commercials, then I was on Broadway, then suddenly I was out in California doing TV." Haywood shook his head and grinned.

"I didn't act in any of the school plays," he added. "I didn't mind not doing that, but I would have liked to be on the school teams. I especially liked basketball, soccer, and track. There just wasn't time when I was working.

Haywood Nelson says his career " . . . happened so *fast.* I did commercials, then I was on Broadway, then suddenly I was out in California doing TV!"

"The kids in school didn't treat me any differently because of my work," Haywood said. "They just knew there were times when I couldn't go to the beach with them because I was working. I wasn't big-headed and didn't feel that I was better than anyone else. There were times, in fact, when I would rather have gone swimming than to work, but something kept me going. For one thing, I saw how hard it was for other kids to get jobs. I thought to myself: I have a job now. I'd better stay with it."

Haywood laughed, remembering those days. "One time when I was appearing on Broadway," he said, "I was really sick with a cold and I had twisted my ankle, so I couldn't walk or talk. But they couldn't find my understudy, so I had to go in to work and I was *miserable*. It was a good experience, though," he admitted.

"Working on Broadway helped me a great deal. If I hadn't been on Broadway, I don't think I'd appreciate being in *What's Happening!!* Once you do Broadway, you see how much easier TV is. When you make a mistake on the stage, you can't say, 'Stop, let's do it again.'"

Haywood got the part in *What's Happening!!* before he had graduated from high school. Taking the job meant working on the West Coast, so the family split up temporarily. Haywood and his mother headed west and lived in an apartment during the first two years of the series. "We were back and forth between New York and California a lot," Haywood laughed. "Finally Dad and Gary moved to California. Dad is working for a travel agent now. They moved into a new house last summer. I lived at home until then. I always had to help around the house by doing the dishes and taking care of our dogs. We have two: Gary's is half Siberian husky and half German shepherd. My dog is an Alaskan malamute. We love to take them to the park and let them run."

Haywood admitted that it was hard to go to school and work in a TV series at the same time. "My advice to kids who want to go into this business is to get their schooling out of the way first and then go after their career," he said. "It's hard to do both. For the first year and a half on the show, I had to have a tutor on the set, and I had a tutor I didn't like. She was used to teaching younger kids. I was in the 11th grade and she had me doing little kiddie exercises. I finally went back to Long Island and finished high school there. I graduated from Mineola High School in 1977. Now I can work without having to go to school at the same time."

In addition to acting, Haywood loves art. "I'd like to go to night school and take commercial art and design," he said. "I like to draw and sketch

Haywood Nelson (Dwayne), Fred Berry (Rerun), and Ernest Thomas (Raj) play high-school friends on the popular *What's Happening!!* Between the three of them, the audience never knows *what* to expect!

with a pencil, then add color with a magic marker. I wouldn't want to give up acting, but I'd also like to get into commercial art."

Haywood also enjoys music and he loves to dance.

Haywood says that his family has always been very helpful to him in his career. "My mother always said I could quit working if I wanted to. There were times when I threatened to quit, but I didn't really want to. Now my family tries to help me with the mail I get. There's so much of it I can't keep up!"

What about social life, I asked. Does your work allow you time for that? "I don't have many friends in California," Haywood said, "but I have some. We go to the beach or we go surfing, horseback riding or we play basketball.

"But, you know," Haywood said with a grin, "I really get bored when I'm not working. When I'm not working, I wake up, look at a wall, and think, 'Well, what shall I do today?'"

But today Haywood had already solved his problem. When we finished our interview he would take off for an afternoon of surfing!

## ☆ Melissa Gilbert and Melissa Sue Anderson: ☆ "Melissa Sisters" on *Little House on the Prairie*

Scene: High noon on the main street of an old Western town. Horses hitched to wagons are standing quietly in the bright sunshine. People, dressed in old-fashioned clothes, huddle together in the few spots of shade. It is hot and dusty.

The horses, the heat, and the people were real. The town was not. I was in Hollywood, and this was the set for NBC's *Little House on the Prairie*. I was to have lunch with Melissa Gilbert who plays Laura Ingalls in the popular series.

Melissa was standing on the corner of the street, listening to Michael Landon. He was telling her what to do in the next scene. Michael plays Pa Ingalls in the series. He also writes and directs

Mary (Melissa Sue Anderson) and Pa Ingalls (Michael Landon) enjoy a quiet talk. When anyone needs help, Pa is always there.

many of the shows. He gave Melissa final instructions and then stepped back. "Quiet, please!" a man called. The cameras began to roll. Melissa stood, talking directly into the camera. Behind her, the men in the wagons began driving their horses into town.

They finished the scene; then they did it over once more. After that, the cast and crew took a break for lunch.

I walked over to the corner where Melissa was standing. She looked hot and tired. "The hardest thing is working in the heat," she said. "I can't take it." She wiped her face with her hand and smiled.

She had an hour for lunch, and we headed inside where it was cool. Melissa ordered a hamburger and two glasses of orange juice.

Melissa has played Laura Ingalls for four years. "I love acting," she said. "I never get tired of it."

She began acting when she was three. "I did a commercial for baby clothes," she recalled. She is 14 now and has never had acting lessons, but she has learned a lot.

"I've always loved horses," she said. "And the wranglers on the show taught me how to ride. And stunt men showed me how to act out a fight. That's fun to do," she added enthusiastically. "It's easier to give the punch than it is to take the punch. When you're the one getting hit, you wait until you see the fist in front of your face. Then you throw your head aside and throw yourself on the ground. It looks like you've been hit, but you haven't been touched at all!" Melissa laughed.

Sometimes Melissa has to laugh or cry in a scene. "Crying is easy," she told me. "You just think of something sad. Then you cry. I think of sad things that could happen to my family."

Laughing is harder. "Sometimes you can't think of anything funny," Melissa said. "It's hard to laugh and not sound like you're forcing it. It's especially hard to laugh when you have to do a scene over and over."

"How do you make yourself laugh?" I asked the young actress.

"I imagine everybody in their underwear," she replied with a giggle.

Melissa and the other young people on the show put in busy days. When they are working, they must go to school three hours a day. A teacher comes to the set. "One minute we're working, the next minute we're in school," Melissa said. "When the show isn't in production, I go to regular school. I'm in the 10th grade. I like school a lot, especially algebra. That's my best subject. I've never gotten anything lower than an A in it. This year my courses include history, French, and English."

Melissa's younger brother is also in *Little House*

*on the Prairie*. Jonathan, who is 11 years old, plays
Willie. "We get along very well," Melissa said, just
as Jonathan appeared at our table. He was carrying a luncheon tray. On it were jello, chocolate
milk, two hard-boiled eggs, and a slice of ham.
Melissa looked at it and made a face as Jonathan sat
down with us.

Melissa and Jonathan live with their mother and
stepfather and three-year-old sister in Encino,
California. "Jonathan and I have chores we have to
do around the house," Melissa told me. "We have
to clean our rooms, make our beds, clear the table,
and baby-sit sometimes."

The two get weekly allowances, they said. "I
save mine," Jonathan said.

"I spend mine on everything in sight," Melissa
admitted. "I like to buy presents for people. I buy
my mother flowers—especially when I'm in trouble with her! That only happens when I do things
like forget to clean my room or lose my retainer."

Melissa and Jonathan like sports of all kinds.
"And I have a big doll house," Melissa said. "I
collect miniatures for that. When we're on the set,
and not working or going to school, we play
backgammon, cards, checkers, and other games.
But I don't have much free time during the working day."

Melissa has no trouble learning her lines for the

show, she said. "I study my lines in the car on the way home. It doesn't take me very long. I don't work on them again until I get back on the set the next day. Then I go over the script once or twice to make sure I know what I'm doing.

"Once," Melissa added, looking upset, "I really goofed. I kept making mistakes. I had to do one scene over 13 times! I felt *awful*. I was so upset I started to cry. Luckily, my mother was there that day and she calmed me down. We don't have many goof-ups on the set. People forget lines sometimes, but that's about all."

Michael Landon, Melissa said, has been very helpful to everybody in the show. "He's just like a father to me. He's a lot of fun to be around. He's always telling jokes," she said.

I asked Melissa how she would describe Laura Ingalls. "She is just like me! Laura is a fun, outgoing girl who enjoys animals and likes being with people," Melissa replied. "She is kind of a tomboy. I have a lot of fun playing her. Mary (played by Melissa Sue Anderson) is more prim and proper."

Melissa never gets bored working or feels that she is missing out on anything by working. "I hope to continue acting forever!" she exclaimed.

By the time our luncheon was over and we headed back to the set, the sun was hotter than ever. Everybody was back on the dusty Western

Laura (Melissa Gilbert) spends one school recess playing baseball, while younger sister Carrie (Lindsey Greenbush) watches from a safe distance!

street. The horses looked sleepy, but all the people appeared to be wide-awake. Melissa Gilbert went back to work, just as Melissa Sue Anderson came walking up the street. Melissa Sue Anderson wasn't needed in the scene right then, so she stopped to talk. As Mary Ingalls in the series, she loves *everything* about the show — except wearing old-fashioned dresses and high-button shoes! "Someday I'd like to do a TV series that *isn't* a Western set in the 1800's," she laughed.

Melissa Sue Anderson is 16. She got her start in show business by doing TV commercials. And she'll never forget the day she did her first commercial. "It was for a toy company," she recalled. "I was terrified! You do commercials over and over. Sometimes you shoot a 30-second commercial more than 50 times! Somehow, I managed to do it."

Melissa has never taken acting lessons. "I've learned from watching others and from being in *Little House on the Prairie*," she said. "I usually spend about ten minutes a day learning my lines. I go over them at night just before my head hits the pillow. Then, if I'm lucky, the words just flow out of my mouth the next day."

Does she get tired of playing the same role? Melissa smiled at the question. "I get tired of it sometimes," she replied, "but mostly I enjoy it.

It's nice to know you have a job. It's like having a teddy bear — it's something steady you can depend on!"

Melissa lives in an apartment with her mother and her dog, Barney, a Lhasa apso. "Once I leave the studio at the end of the day, I try to leave 'show business' behind," Melissa said. "Most of my friends are not in the business. And it's a relief to get into my own clothes, especially jeans, which I prefer."

Melissa has high hopes for the future and one dream: "To keep on acting" — even if it does mean wearing old-fashioned dresses and bonnets!

## ☆ Parker Stevenson and Shaun Cassidy: ☆ Keeping Up With *The Hardy Boys*

As I drove out to see Parker Stevenson, I reminded myself that he and co-star Shaun Cassidy were enjoying a break before taping the newest episodes of *The Hardy Boys Mysteries*. The two TV brothers are every bit as busy with their own activities as they are when their popular show is in production.

On the day I went to see him, Parker was playing in a tennis tournament at a beautiful country club in Los Angeles. Many of the players were businessmen who had paid a fee to play tennis with Hollywood celebrities. Proceeds from the tournament were to go to a charity for young people.

Parker finished the game he was playing. Then he came over to talk for awhile before being called back on the court. "This is the first time I've played in this tournament," he said with a smile as he sat beside me on a bench overlooking the tennis courts. "When they asked me to play, I told them I was out of practice. I played a lot as a kid. Now I have to get back into practice and improve my game."

Parker had just returned to the West Coast from a trip to New York. He had visited his parents in Westchester County, where he grew up. He had danced at a disco on Park Avenue, taken part in the opening of a new film, and just generally "organized my life," he laughed.

While Parker was doing all that, Shaun Cassidy was on the road. He had just begun a 19-city concert tour and was being mobbed by young fans everywhere he went.

"Shaun and I get along so well," Parker said. "We are very different people with different temperaments, and that's good. There is no feeling of competition between us. We each get about 10,000 letters a week. There's no way we can read all that mail! I used to try to answer all my mail myself. Now the studio does it for me. I couldn't keep up with it. Neither can Shaun. His records and concerts don't allow him much free time!"

Parker is pleased that ABC renewed *The Hardy Boys Mysteries* this season. "I think the TV show has gotten better," he said. "The stories have gotten better and more exciting. And I think we'll continue to improve. Everybody in the show works very hard. We want it to be a success. The response from young people has been so tremendous. They are our most important audience. We don't want to lose them."

Parker got into show business by doing TV commercials. At one point of his life, he thought he might be an architect. But the acting bug bit him early, and he never quite recovered. The producers of *The Hardy Boys Mysteries* saw him in a movie called *Lifeguard*. The movie wasn't exactly outstanding, but Parker himself was.

*"The Hardy Boys'* producers asked me to fly out to Hollywood to try out for a part in their new TV series," Parker recalled. "Shaun Cassidy was the first one they had tested. I was the last. I tested with Shaun and I thought I was *terrible*! Sometimes you feel good about something you've done — and sometimes you don't.

"After I made the screen test, I went home to New York. A week later they called me and said they wanted to film a brief presentation to show network executives. So I flew back to California. We spent one day filming the presentation, and then we went right into production. It was wild! I thought I was going to California for three days — and I stayed. It was an amazing experience!"

Parker had read many of the Hardy Boys books when he was growing up. He reread some of them after he got the part of the older brother, Frank Hardy. "The stories are so good! At first I wasn't sure I wanted to do a TV series," he said. "A series can be a long-term commitment. An actor might end up being in a successful series for *years*. But how could I turn down *The Hardy Boys*? Frank and Joe Hardy are very special. They are very all-American — clean-cut, adventurous, bright young men. The fact that their father is a detective makes their adventures seem realistic. There are so many things that can be done with the two brothers and their relationship. The fun of the show comes from the danger the Hardys get into and their reaction to that danger."

Parker hopes that, in his words, "the show will be a stepping-stone toward all I want to do in the future. I want to learn editing and directing and all about TV production."

"I'd also like to do a TV movie or a feature film," Parker added. "It would be fun to have more time to work on a role. We have to crank out *The Hardy Boys* so fast that we have little time to develop our characters. I guess that's good in one sense, though, because it really keeps us on our toes."

At first, Parker Stevenson wasn't sure he wanted to star in a TV series, because "an actor might end up being in a successful series for *years.* But how could I turn down *The Hardy Boys*?!"

Parker was needed on his toes right then — back on the tennis court. He grinned and picked up his racket. Parker is a young man of great intelligence and appeal. He is bright and friendly. He is, in fact, just like the all-American Frank Hardy!

His co-star, Shaun Cassidy, is 20 years old, and one of the hottest young stars in the world. Shaun's first two records sold more than five million copies. His concerts are sell-outs. Sales of Shaun Cassidy wristwatches and lunch boxes and posters are booming.

All of that is tremendously exciting for a young man, but Shaun is taking it in stride. He has been around show business all his life and has seen its ups and downs. His mother is actress Shirley Jones, who was in *The Partridge Family* on TV. His father, actor Jack Cassidy, was killed in an apartment fire several years ago. "The biggest disappointment in my life," Shaun told me, "is that my father never got to hear me perform. I think he would have been proud of what I've accomplished."

Shaun grew up in Beverly Hills, California, with his parents and two younger brothers, Patrick, now 16, and Ryan, 12. His half-brother, David Cassidy, grew up in New Jersey with his mother, actress Evelyn Ward.

In addition to his success on *The Hardy Boys,* Shaun's singing career has skyrocketed.

Shaun graduated from high school in June, 1976. "I had a band in high school," he said. "We played for dances and parties. I was always busy with music and acting. I couldn't stand things like football games! I started touring with my mother when I was about 14. She was doing summer stock productions of musicals. I got small roles in several of them, including *Oliver* and *The Sound of Music*. That was my first taste of being on the road.

"I've always been very close to my mother," Shaun added. "She was so family-oriented. It's hard to understand why she went into show business in the first place. She was not a show business mother at all. She knew everything my brothers and I were doing. She disciplined us and guided us."

It was David who gave Shaun a firsthand look at the dizzying effects of a pop career. David, now 28, was also in *The Partridge Family*. He became a teen idol because of that TV show and he turned his popularity into a rock music career that was brief — but frantic. He was swamped by fans in concert tours around the world — just as Shaun is now. Then his music career fizzled, and David moved on to other things.

"Seeing David's career was a great experience for me," Shaun said. "I learned that this whole thing is a business and that's how you must treat it.

I was a senior in high school when I went on my first European singing tour. My parents wanted me to wait until I had finished high school, but I knew what I was getting into. I had seen how David's career had gone and I had seen my parents' ups and downs."

Being a pop star has some disadvantages, Shaun has discovered. "I have little privacy," he noted. "I like to go places and not be recognized, but that's a thing of the past. And I have little free time now.

"I've always been a very conservative person," Shaun said. "When I was in school, I couldn't understand the wild, crazy kids. I was calm. But I was happy all the time. I enjoyed myself." Shaun laughed. "I believe in enjoying myself," he added. "The minute I stop enjoying my work, I won't do it any longer. So many people in show business work hard to be successful. The minute they become successful, they go into hiding. That amazes me! Success doesn't last forever. Why not enjoy it?

"I did some acting in school plays," Shaun noted. "But I was hesitant about doing *The Hardy Boys* when it first came up. I said, 'I'm a singer, not an actor.' My music career was going well in Europe — and the idea of a regular job worried me. But there's no doubt that TV played a big part in the success of 'Da Doo Ron Ron,' my first single."

Shaun knows that pop careers can be brief and he is already making big plans for the next few years. "I want to record many more songs," he said eagerly. "And I want to write and get into the production end of this whole business."

At 20, he's a singing sensation, a TV star, an actor and a song writer. By the time he's 21, who knows what new careers Shaun Cassidy will have added to his life?

Joe Hardy (Shaun Cassidy), Nancy Drew (Janet Louise Johnson), and Frank Hardy (Parker Stevenson). The Hardy Boys and Nancy Drew frequently combine their detective talents when they have a particularly tough case to crack.

# ☆ John Travolta: ☆ Superstardom for *Welcome Back, Kotter's* Favorite Sweathog

John Travolta wasn't a star when I first met him. He was a young, unknown actor who had been signed to play a role in a new TV series called *Welcome Back, Kotter.* That was in the summer of 1975. *Welcome Back, Kotter* had not come on the air. ABC believed that John was an actor with great deal of appeal, but few reporters had interviewed him. No one knew much about him. But interviewing young performers is part of my job. Who knows? Maybe one of them will turn out to be the star of a new hit show — or even become a big star in his (or her) own name, as Travolta has done.

Few performers ever do achieve stardom. Show business is tough. Success requires talent, determination, hard work — and an incredible amount of luck. And getting the right role at the right time is of great importance too. John Travolta has gotten those roles, beginning with that of Vinnie Barbarino in *Welcome Back, Kotter*. And he has become a star — one of the biggest stars of his time.

John was nominated for an Academy Award for his sensational performance in *Saturday Night Fever*. And he hit movie theaters like a bolt of greased lightning with his performance in the film version of the Broadway musical, *Grease*. He is signed to do more movies, at about one million dollars per movie. He now has an agent, publicist, manager, financial adviser, secretary, and lawyer.

But three years ago, he had only himself and his high hopes for the success of *Welcome Back, Kotter*. He had been acting for years. He knew that co-starring in a TV series would give him valuable national exposure. When we sat in a small coffee shop in West Hollywood in 1975, John talked quietly about himself and his hopes for the future. Of the other young actors and actresses who sat at tables around us, no one could have guessed that out of them all, it would be John Travolta who would become a superstar.

That day John told me about growing up in Englewood, New Jersey. He was one of six children. Helen and Sam Travolta were their parents.

"I've worked from the time I was 12. My first job

John as he appeared in the smash movie "Saturday Night Fever." His TV career has lead to starring roles in movies and recording hit songs.

was as a carpenter's helper," John said. "I put fabric on chairs and rebuilt tables."

John started acting at the encouragement of his mother, who had been active as a teacher, director, and actress for 20 years. He quit high school in his junior year to become a full-time actor.

"I was doing summer stock then, and I was working too much to go to school at the same time," John explained. "I wanted to work. I enjoyed it. I just like everything about it! At first there was a little tension with my parents, but my interest was so strong. My mother understood what I wanted to do. I was 16. My three older sisters were all actresses. I had grown up watching them go through the problems of their acting careers. I saw a lot of shows and plays. It was a natural thing. Acting was all around me.

"My father is retired now. Then he owned a business in Hillsdale. He had been a semi-pro basketball player. My mother directed a stock company in Englewood and did all kinds of things. She was going all the time. My family life was very good. My father enjoyed all of our careers. He went to all the plays we were in. Both my parents were totally interested in everything we did. My brothers were athletes, so they went to their games, too.

"I got involved in community theater as a child," John recalled. "When I was 14 I started going to New York to audition for professional parts. My first professional job was in summer stock in New Jersey. That was at the end of my sophomore year in high school."

Summer stock changed everything for John. "Before that I lived a normal life. I had regular friends and buddies. We played sports. I played basketball and football in junior high. But gradually one job led to another — and the jobs began to overlap with school. I couldn't do both and I wanted to work."

Following his job with a summer stock company, John played in a revival of *Rain* in an off-Broadway production. He also got a minor role in the roadshow company of *Grease*. "We toured all over the country," he said. "I also did *Grease* on Broadway and was in *Over Here* with the Andrews sisters for nine months."

John moved to Los Angeles in 1972, when he was 18 years old. For several years he did TV commercials and made the rounds looking for acting jobs. Then along came *Kotter*, and the spark was lighted. The world was about to hear from a rising young star named John Travolta.

"Being an actor," John admitted, "is a good life. I have time to spend with my airplane and with people I like. I travel a lot and I enjoy it all."

John doesn't believe he missed out on anything by starting to act when he was so young. "When I was 14 and 15," he said, "I always tried to have something going. When I wasn't playing basketball or acting or doing something, I fell apart. It's better to have something to do. It's tough to be a teenager. You are facing a whole life ahead of you and you don't always know what you want to do with that life."

John knew, however. He wanted to be an actor. Now, acting offers are pouring in from all over, and John is still under contract to appear in *Welcome Back, Kotter*. He is no longer in every episode, but was scheduled to make about eight appearances this season. John's interests and talents may have moved far beyond the sweathogs and Mr. Kotter's classroom. He realizes, however, that the role of Vinnie Barbarino first got his career off the ground. "I love slipping into the role of Barbarino," he said. "I think it's hilarious when people call me Barbarino and react to me as if I were him. I guess it's a compliment to my acting ability. Fortunately, the people in the industry know I can do something else beside Vinnie Barbarino."

Some people have suggested that John may be a flash-in-the-pan pop success — big today and forgotten tomorrow. John himself is convinced that

John Travolta as Vinnie Barbarino. "I think it's hilarious when people call me Barbarino," he said. "I guess it's a compliment to my acting ability."

won't happen. "It's hard to be a flash-in-the-pan when your career is booked for the next three years," he told one reporter. "I have records, movies, and television commitments — that's an awfully long flash!"

John Travolta has come a long way since I met him at that coffee shop in West Hollywood in 1975. And John has handled his success well. His career may be in orbit, but his feet are on the ground. He has remained close to his family in New Jersey and he has tried to plan carefully for the future.

## ☆ Beyond This Planet Earth: ☆ Mork and Mindy, Project U.F.O., and *Battlestar Galactica*

There's a lot going on in outer space these days — if you can believe what you see on TV! The planet Ork has sent an observer to earth. UFO's are coming at us from all directions in *Project U.F.O.* And the *Battlestar Galactica* is loaded with people traveling through outer space trying to find a safe place to live.

The networks have high hopes for their science fiction shows. Let's take a look at the shows and some of the people in them.

### Mork And Mindy

Last season, a new character appeared on *Happy Days*. He wasn't even from this planet! He was Mork from the planet Ork. He appeared to

Richie Cunningham one night in a dream. Or was it a dream? Richie didn't think so and he was right. Mork is back again this year with his *own* TV show on ABC.

Mork lives in Boulder, Colorado. He has come because his fellow Orkans believe they will have to abandon their planet one day. Mork is an explorer who has been assigned to investigate Earth as a possible place for the Orkans to relocate.

It's a tricky assignment. Mork's success on Earth depends on his ability to keep his true identity a secret. He must blend in and function as a member of Earth society so that he can accurately report back to Ork.

Mork has one friend who knows he's not an everyday earthling. Her name is Mindy, a charming 21-year-old who works in her grandmother's music store. Mindy also works hard at helping Mork keep his cover. One of her main jobs is to teach Mork the meaning of such expressions as "Go jump in the lake" or "Get lost." Without Mindy, Mork would go looking for a lake to jump into!

Producer Garry Marshall picked a young stand-up comedian named Robin Williams to play Mork. Mindy, his co-star, is played by actress Pam Dawber. Pam wasn't in town the day I talked to Robin. Robin, however, talked eagerly about his role and his career.

Mork with one of his favorite snacks: fresh flowers!

Robin was born in Scotland and lived there for a year as a child. His father was an executive for the Ford Motor Company. "When we came back from Scotland, the company moved him back and forth between Chicago and Detroit," Robin recalled. "I kept changing schools as we moved around. Then, when I was in high school, my father retired and we moved to San Francisco. I loved it there. I used to go to a place called The Committee where you could watch young comedians try out their material. I wasn't really thinking of performing myself. I just liked watching them."

The idea of performing began to seem more and more appealing to him. Although he enrolled at a local college, planning to major in political science, he stayed with that for only a year. Then he headed for New York to study acting.

"I went to a fine acting school where they taught everything — juggling, gymnastics, mask work, theater history...and improvisational theater (working without a script)," Robin said. "Improvisational theater led me, eventually, to doing stand-up comedy."

At one time, he and a friend performed as mimes in New York's famous Central Park. Each day they painted their faces white, put on costumes, and headed for the park. "People of all ages stopped to watch us perform," Robin said. "We did it to earn money. It seemed like the right kind of work for us, since we were both going to acting school at the time. A group of us lived together and we didn't have much. We ate a lot of cottage cheese, yogurt, and cheese sandwiches."

After he finished acting school, Robin headed home to San Francisco. He wanted to put his lessons to work. He wanted to act. "But there was only one acting company in town," Robin said, "and they weren't holding auditions. So one night I went to a comedy workshop and began to work there regularly. In the workshop we'd have classes and perform for each other. Then we'd perform for the public. We didn't get paid, so I had to take other jobs, such as being a waiter and a housepainter.

"Since then, I have worked as a stand-up comic in a number of clubs. Most of them don't pay you. They figure they are doing you a favor by letting you perform. I've really worked in some awful places," Robin said with a shudder. "I've performed in discos — while they were still dancing! Or my act has been sandwiched between two rock 'n' roll bands...You go through those times, telling yourself, 'I'll live' — and hoping you will! You just try to keep moving on to better clubs."

Robin kept moving and trying to improve his comedy. "You have to find your own style," he

Robin Williams and Pam Dawber star in *Mork and Mindy.* Mindy never *dreamed* it would be such a challenge to teach Mork how to behave like an everyday Earthling!

noted. "I do all kinds of crazy characters in my act. I do a Russian comedian, Nicky Lenin; a five-year-old nuclear scientist; an old hippy poet called Grandpa Funk, and so on."

The week before he tried out for the role of Mork in the *Happy Days* episode, Robin saw the movie, *Close Encounters of the Third Kind*. "After I saw that, I decided to add a new character to my act called the Alien Comedian," Robin laughed. "The Alien Comedian talks gibberish. When I walked in to read for the part of Mork I saw that the script called for him to use crazy sound effects — beeps, noises, etc.! That's just what I had been doing in my act!" Small wonder that Robin got the part of Mork from Ork in *Happy Days*!

As for his own show, an offbeat comedy is always a gamble. But who would have thought that two factory girls (*Laverne and Shirley*) or a tough motorcycle rider (*Happy Days*) would make two of the greatest hit shows of all time? Whether Mork from Ork outlives this season or not, we can be sure that we'll hear more than gibberish and beeping from the talented young comedian, Robin Williams.

## Project U.F.O.

Do UFO's really exist? Many people believe they do. For many years now, people around the world have reported seeing unidentified flying objects in the air — objects of all different colors, sizes, and shapes; objects making different kinds of sounds, from whirrings and whinings to bumpings and beepings.

Last spring, NBC came up with a new series based on actual reportings of UFO's. Its stories are based on actual cases reported in the files of the Air Force's Project Blue Book.

Project Blue Book was set up by the Air Force to investigate the many reports of UFO sightings that were coming in. It was in operation for 22 years. Then the information it had uncovered was filed away and might have been forgotten. Except that...

Several years ago, Congress passed a law that opened up certain governmental files to the public. TV producer Jack Webb was quick to respond. He wanted to know what was in the files of Project Blue Book. And what he found is being used as the basis of stories for *Project U.F.O.*

Webb obtained microfilm of more than 40,000 documents covering some 13,000 sightings from the files. "About 70 percent of the cases were explained satisfactorily," Webb said. "They were natural phenomena like balloons or clouds. People saw them and thought they were seeing UFO's. There were tricks, too, like people sailing hubcaps in the air and photographing them." But about 15 percent of the reported sightings, Webb said, were never explained. Nobody could prove they were UFO's — but no one could prove they weren't either. Those were the cases that interested Webb.

He was the perfect person to try dramatizing some of those reported sightings. Two of his popular shows, *Dragnet* and *Adam-12*, were based on actual cases taken from the files of the Los Angeles Police Department. Webb believed viewers wanted reality and he tried to give it to them.

He tried to do the same thing in creating *Project U.F.O.* He picked a retired Air Force colonel named William Coleman for his producer. Coleman headed the Blue Book project in the early 1960's. And Webb also helped pick the two actors (Caskey Swaim and Edward Winter) who would play the Air Force investigators sent out to study reports of UFO sightings.

I didn't meet Caskey's partner, played by Edward Winter, but I did get to talk with Caskey Swaim, who has been with *Project U.F.O.* since it started last season.

Being in *Project U.F.O.* is a big step for Caskey Swaim. It is his first TV role. Most actors work their way up from smaller roles. But Caskey *started* his TV career in a starring role! That's not bad for someone who grew up in Lexington, North Carolina. Or for someone who was a bellhop in a Hollywood hotel until a year ago.

"I'd had no acting training when I arrived in Los Angeles," Caskey admitted. "I had done imitations of Andy Griffith and Elvis Presley in local talent shows when I was in the first grade, but that was all!"

Nevertheless, Caskey was determined to be an actor. First, he had to find a job to support himself while he looked for acting jobs — or for acting experience of any kind. That's when he started working as a bellhop at a hotel on Sunset Boulevard. A friend there told him about a group putting on a play at a local theater. He went to join them and discovered that the director of the play was a fellow southerner. The man became his agent, helping Caskey try to get acting jobs.

Caskey got his first role in March, 1977. "It was a small part in Henry Winkler's film, *Heroes*," he recalled. "Then my agent met Jack Webb's casting director, and that led to my getting the part in *Project U.F.O.*"

Caskey has no intention of being overwhelmed by the money and glamour and excitement of being a TV star. "I was a bellhop too long to get carried away with myself now," he said with a smile. "I worked at that hotel for five years and I still keep in touch with the people there."

Ryan (Edward Winter) and Fitz (Caskey Swaim) investigate the site of a reported UFO appearance.

Does he believe in UFO's? Caskey nodded. "The government set up Project Blue Book because they were receiving so many reports of UFO sightings," he replied. "The Air Force wanted to find out what these reported objects were and whether they posed any threat to national security. Some they could explain; others they couldn't.

"Sure, I believe UFO's may exist," the young actor added. "I started believing in them after we put a man on the moon. If we can do that, how can we discount the possibility that there may be other activity going on in outer space? I don't believe we can — or should."

## Battlestar Galactica

ABC's *Battlestar Galactica* is considered by some to be TV's answer to *Star Wars*. Its producer and supervisor of special effects is John Dykstra, who won an Oscar for his fabulous special effects in *Star Wars*. The show has turned out to be one of the costliest and most ambitious TV series ever produced.

It takes place thousands of years in the future, in galaxies far away. Richard Hatch and Dirk Benedict star as two fighter pilots aboard the spaceship *Galactica*, whose commander is played by Lorne Greene.

Dykstra had never worked in TV before, and he

admitted that it was a very different medium from feature films. "It is totally different, in fact," he told me in an interview. We were sitting in an office of his workshop in Van Nuys, California. Back in the workshop itself, his crew was still working on all the models and filming the special effects needed for *Battlestar Galactica*. Dykstra, I knew, was the guiding light behind it all.

"Scale is so different on TV," he explained, "because the TV screen itself is so small. The screen is smaller than the models we build. We've built more than 45 miniature spaceship models."

The starship *Galactica* appears to be about 2,000 feet long when you see it on TV. In reality, Dykstra said, it is 72 inches long and weighs 60 pounds. It's illusion of great size comes from the attention paid to the detail of its surfaces and the hundreds of portholes which glow from inner lighting.

"We also created a robot dog," Dykstra said with a smile. "The dog has no mechanical parts, but I won't tell you how it works." (I learned the secret of the robot dog a few hours after seeing Dykstra, when I went to visit the Galactica set. The robot dog is actually played by a charming *chimp*! In real life, the chimpanzee has his own pet — a little dog! That's what you call a switch!)

Dykstra is one of the special effects geniuses of

Lt. Starbuck (Dirk Benedict), Commander Adama (Lorne Greene), and Captain Apollo (Richard Hatch) star in the exciting *Battlestar Galactica*. These three men are chiefly responsible for the ship Galactica, which is carrying surviving members of the human race to the planet Earth.

today. But no one is more aware than he that special effects alone can't carry a TV show week after week. "The story is still the main thing," he pointed out. "The story is the framework of a show. The action and the visual effects are only fillers. A show can be a success if it's visually good, but it needs a good story to be a really big success."

Dykstra's hope in producing the show was that *Battlestar Galactica* would combine everything — exciting stories, good character development, and special effects that will dazzle your senses.

"It is a sheer joy making things that don't exist," he said of all of his special effects. "I'm actually creating my own reality. Say," he added with a big grin, "would you like to see our workroom?" With that, we walked into a huge room filled with miniature spaceships and strange lights and weird landscapes meant to represent other planets. It was a strange and wonderful experience — even in miniature!

Outer space is a busy place this year. And John Dykstra is filling up the outer space in the TV viewer's eye with his own unique, imaginative space fantasies.